Discussion Guide for Hot Apple Cider

STORIES *to* STIR THE HEART
and WARM THE SOUL

Edited by

N. J. LINDQUIST *and* MARGUERITE CUMMINGS

That's Life! Communications

Markham, Ontario

Discussion Guide for Hot Apple Cider

That's Life! Communications

Box 77001, Markham, ON L3P 0C8, Canada
905-471-1447
http://thatslifecommunications.com
comments@thatslifecommunications.com

ISBN: 978-1-927692-38-7

Copyright © That's Life! Communications 2014, 2016

All rights reserved.

The copyright for all stories, essays, and poems referred to in this book rests with the individual authors.

This study guide is created to be used in conjunction with the book *Hot Apple Cider*.

Without limiting the rights under copyright reserved above, no part of this book may be reproduced, stored in or introduced into a retrieval system, or transmitted, in any form or by any means (electronic, mechanical, photocopying, recording, or otherwise) without the prior written permission of the publisher.

All scripture quotations, unless otherwise indicated, are taken from the HOLY BIBLE, NEW INTERNATIONAL VERSION®. NIV®. Copyright © 1973, 1978, 1984, 2011 by Biblica, Inc.™ Used by permission of Zondervan. All rights reserved.

Cover design and interior layout for this book by N. J. Lindquist.
Cover design for *Hot Apple Cider* by Ingrid Paulson (Ingrid Paulson Design).
Photo illustrations were acquired from iStockphoto.

Publisher's Note: The scanning, uploading, and distribution of this book via the Internet or via any other means without the permission of the publisher is illegal and punishable by law. Please purchase only authorized editions, and do not participate in, or encourage, piracy of copyrighted materials.

Your support of the authors' rights is appreciated.

About This Discussion Guide

Purpose

This guide is intended as a companion to the book *Hot Apple Cider*, an award-winning collection of 44 stories of hope and encouragement.

Trade paperback and digital

If you don't have your own copy of this book, you can get a print copy from most bookstores or directly from the publisher, That's Life! Communications. Or you can get an e-book from most e-book retailers.

Leaders of small groups can place bulk orders at a much-reduced rate from That's Life! Communications.

More information at:

http://hotappleciderbooks.com

Structure

This guide follows essentially the same structure as the original book. For each of the 44 stories, we've provided a set of in-depth discussion questions to help you:

- Think further about the issues raised
- Enjoy stimulating conversations
- Share ideas and meaningful experiences

Who should use this guide?

This guide is a perfect tool either for private study or for study within a group:

- **Individual Readers:** If you are reading or have read *Hot Apple Cider*, you can use the questions in this guide to meditate on the issues raised by each article, then write down your responses.
- **Book Clubs:** *Hot Apple Cider* is a great choice for book clubs. With 44 pieces by 30 authors from across Canada, the anthology is so diverse that everyone in your book club is bound to find something enjoyable. Also, the pieces are short, so you can easily talk about a number of them in one evening. Book club leaders can use some or all of the questions in this guide to drive the discussion about each piece.
- **Small Groups:** Whichever kind of small group you are in—a discussion group, adult class, men's or women's group, or a support group for people facing issues such as illness or bereavement—you'll find material that will interest and benefit the members of your group. Many stories and questions include Scripture references.
- **Speakers, Pastors, Teachers:** The stories in *Hot Apple Cider* provide wonderful material for a talk, sermon, devotional, or group discussion. The questions in this

guide are designed to give you insights and often additional Scripture references that you can use in your talk.

How to use this guide

- This guide assumes that you have *Hot Apple Cider* close at hand, whether in print form or as an e-book.
- Some questions include Scripture references, so you may want to have access to a Bible as well.
- Where quoted, verses are taken from the New International Version of the Bible (NIV).
- Make sure you take a look at our free *Reader's Guide for Hot Apple Cider.* This is an ideal tool to give you an overview of the book and its key topics. It can also help you select stories based on their content and length. See the next page for more information.

Reader's Guide

We know you're busy, so to help you select stories quickly, we've created a free, concise (2-page) *Reader's Guide for Hot Apple Cider*, with:

- A list of key topics addressed in the book
- A short description of each piece
- The length of each story (page numbers in print book)
- The approximate time it takes to read each story aloud

A downloadable 2-page PDF (legal size) of the *Reader's Guide* is available at:

> http://thatslifecommunications.com/ hot-apple-cider-books/ study-helps/

Note: The *Reader's Guide* works best when printed double-sided on legal paper and folded into a pamphlet. If you would like to print it, make sure you follow the instructions on the website.

Reader's Guide for *Hot Apple Cider*

Winner of 6 awards, including Church Library Association of Ontario "One Book/One Conference"

Enjoy 44 stories of hope in this award-winning bestseller!

"Highly recommended"
Midwest Book Review

http://hotapplaciderbooks.com

Alternatively, you can get **free printed copies** from That's Life! Communications with any book order.

Note: Please also check out the "Index of Authors and Discussion Pages" on pages 104 and 105 of this book.

Connect with the Writers & Editors

Most of the writers and editors whose work is included in *Hot Apple Cider* are experienced public speakers. They can address the topics they've written about in the book, and they have other interests as well. Please check their websites to find out where they're based and learn more about their writing and expertise.

Many are available for bookings to speak or read from their work; most would be willing to do a telephone or Skype conversation with a small group; some might be involved in future webinars (online seminars, panels, or discussions).

If you'd like to get in touch with some of the writers or editors, try their websites first. See the biographies of contributors at the back of the *Hot Apple Cider* book or visit the contributor page of our website:

http://thatslifecommunications.com/hot-apple-cider-books/hac1writers/

There's also a section at the end of this discussion guide called "Keep in Touch" that will tell you how to subscribe to our newsletter and become part of our community.

Contents

It Was Then That I Carried You *by Angelina Fast-Vlaar* 10
Faith of Our Mothers—Holy Faith *by Keith Clemons* 12
The Diamond Ring *by N. J. Lindquist* 14
An Almost Silent Friendship *by Marcia Lee Laycock* 16
Blind Date *by Paul H. Boge* 18
Romance Amid Reality *by Sheila Wray Gregoire* 20
A Prairie Storm *by Carolyn Arends* 22
The Neatness Wars *by Eric E. Wright* 24
What Your Sock Drawer Says About You *by Sheila Wray Gregoire* 26
Faith, Hope and Love: Give Them A Chance... *by Denyse O'Leary* 28
Nitroglycerin *by Brian C. Austin* 30
Our Kids: Enemies, Allies, or What? *by Ron Wyse* 32
Perspective *by Mark Buchanan* 34
What Was God Thinking? *by Brad Burke, MD* 36
Hurtled into the Valley *by Angelina Fast-Vlaar* 38
People Matter Most *by Grace Fox* 40
Broken Bodies, Shattered Lives *by Paul M. Beckingham* 42
Be the CEO of Your Emotions *by Donna Carter* 44
Living Outside Our Comfort Zones *by Eleanor Shepherd* 46
Dylan *by Brian C. Austin* 48
How Big Is Your Umbrella? *by Sheila Wray Gregoire* 50
Jesus' Disciple Wears a Stethoscope *by W. Harold Fuller* 52
Shards of Silence/Seasons of Hope *by M. D. Meyer* 54
Crisis and Character *by Paul M. Beckingham* 56
Searching For Something That Fits *by Marcia Lee Laycock* 58
Friday, 8:50 a.m., April 7, AD 30 *by David Kitz* 60
A Fertile Heart *by Keturah Leonforde* 62
The Joys and Surprises of Giving *by Diane Roblin-Lee* 64
Where Have All the Mothers Gone? *by Thomas Froese/Jean Chamberlain Froese, MD* 66
Mama Nellie *by Paul M. Beckingham* 68
Will My Baby Die Without Me? *by Grace Fox* 70
Jessie's Generation: Canada's Firebrands of Mercy and Justice *by Jane Harris-Zsovan* 72
How I Found Jesus in a Drug Dealer's Apartment *by Deborah Gyapong* 74
Of Cobras, Culture and Change *by Don Ranney, MD, and Ray Wiseman* 76
The Pink Blossom *by Eric E. Wright* 78
The Ventilation Grate *by Brian C. Austin* 80
One True Friend *by Donna Dawson* 82
Padre, Can I Have a Word? *by Paul M. Beckingham* 84
Shared Tears *by Brian C. Austin* 86
On Writing with Passion and Integrity *by M. D. Meyer* 88
My Letter to the Editor *by N. J. Lindquist* 90
The Child on the Tracks *by Carmen Wittmeier* 92
The Stuckville Café *by Bonnie Grove* 94
The Clay and the Vine *by Brian C. Austin* 96
Acknowledgements 99
More Hot Apple Cider books 100
Index of Authors and Discussion pages 104

"It Was Then That I Carried You"

by Angelina Fast-Vlaar

Alone in the Australian outback, a middle-aged woman discovers her husband lying comatose beside her.

Page 15 in print book

1. In this story, Angelina goes through a traumatic experience, losing someone very close to her.

    a) If you've suffered the loss of a loved one, think back to the experience. What did you find most difficult to deal with?

    b) If other people supported you, how did they help?

    c) What one thing was most helpful in your journey toward healing?

2. Angelina received help from several very special people in this story, whom she calls "angels." The angels in this story seemed to say and do just the right thing.

    a) In what ways do you think the use of the word angels here is appropriate or inappropriate?

b) Can you share about a time in your life when God sent you to help someone else in his or her time of need?

c) What are some other ways we can help people in a time of need or loss?

d) What might be some things it's best not to say or do?

3. In his sermon, "God's Purpose in the Storm," Dr. Charles Stanley said, "When God breaks your heart He makes you useful, but He also props open the door of your heart. You become very sensitive to people around you who are hurting." How does this resonate with you?

"Faith of Our Mothers—Holy Faith"

 *by Keith Clemons*

A true story about two miracles—both answers to prayer—involving the author's parents.

Page 25 in print book

1. Keith describes two incidents which he calls "miracles": his dad Sunny's flying experience and his sister Christine's recovery from appendicitis. He attributes both to the prayers of his grandmother and mother, respectively.

   a) Which of these stories did you find easier to accept as being a miracle and not just a coincidence?

   b) What would you say are the differences between the miraculous and the purely coincidental?

2. Have you (or has someone close to you) experienced an answer to prayer that you would call a "miracle"? If so, while respecting the privacy of others, are you able to share all or part of the story?

3. Some people say they believe in miracles, but don't think they've ever experienced one. How might you respond?

4. Sometimes people pray for a miracle and their prayer seems to go unanswered. Why might this happen?

5. How important do you feel it is for parents and grandparents to pray for their children/grandchildren? (A possible resource is http://www.momsinprayer.org.)

"The Diamond Ring"

by N. J. Lindquist

An 80-year-old stranger brings a glimpse of a new world into the life of a lonely young girl.

Page 35 in print book

1. When N. J. was young, she saw herself as the "ugly duckling" in the Hans Christian Andersen fairy tale.

   a) Have you ever felt that you were an ugly duckling?

   b) What happened to help you see yourself as a swan? Or do you still wonder which you are?

2. N. J. eventually decided that one of the reasons she saw herself in a negative way was because she was what is called "gifted" intellectually, and simply didn't fit in well with others.

   a) Is this something you can relate to in any way?

   b) How do you think people labelled as "gifted" are generally perceived?

14   Discussion Guide for Hot Apple Cider

c) What do you think of the label "gifted"?

d) There are some who assume that people who are identified as gifted have it easier in school or in life than others. How might you explain to them that this isn't necessarily true?

3. How do you cope when you feel that other people don't seem to see you the way you see yourself?

4. What steps could you take to try to understand someone else who seems to be very different from you?

5. An elderly stranger had an unexpected effect on N. J.'s life. Can you think of someone—maybe someone unexpected—who had an impact on your life for the better?

"An Almost Silent Friendship"

 **by Marcia Lee Laycock**

*A shy young woman from the Yukon discovers
what it means to be part of God's family.*

Page 41 in print book

1. Marcia doesn't tell us how she became a Christian, but we do know she was an adult, and she lived in a part of the Yukon where there weren't a lot of people, or other Christians. In what ways can you relate to her feelings of insecurity as she adjusted to a new culture?

2. Marcia's original idea of a retreat was just the opposite of what actually happened. Can you share a similar, positive experience where something you were dreading turned out to be much better than you expected?

3. Has a stranger ever helped or prayed for you as Lorna helped Marcia? If so, what happened?

4. How has God used you in a "divine appointment" to help someone else?

5. Share an experience that made you realize how valuable friendships are.

6. What are a few things you could do to be a friend to someone you've recently met?

"Blind Date"

by Paul H. Boge

A young woman who is afraid she may never meet "Mr. Right" learns a lesson of value for anyone.

Page 44 in print book

1. How would you describe your search for a spouse (either in the past or present)?

2. Some people believe there is one perfect person for each of us. In what ways do you agree or disagree?

3. What advice would you give to someone who seems so desperate to find a life partner that he or she might settle for someone who clearly isn't suitable?

4. How do we find the perfect balance between changing (in the hope that we'll attract the right person) and being true to who we are (in the hope that we'll find someone who loves us exactly as we are)?

5. In what ways might God intervene in our lives to help us find the right spouse?

6. What encouragement could you give to someone who is looking for a spouse?

7. At what point does a single person need to accept that singleness might be God's will for him/her?

"Romance Amid Reality"

by Sheila Wray Gregoire

A few tips on breaking down the walls of miscommunication between men and women.

Page 54 in print book

1. Sheila states that one of the biggest barriers to romance is a "tendency we all have to build walls between us because basically we're all insecure" (page 54 in print book).

   a) Do you agree with her?

   b) Why or why not?

   c) What are some other barriers to romance?

2. When we're insecure, we often feel uncomfortable.

   a) At such times, how can we help our spouse or significant other feel more secure and therefore more relaxed?

b) How can we help our children, friends, or co-workers, feel secure?

3. Have you ever argued with someone because he or she assumed you were angry, when you really weren't angry at all? If so, what happened?

4. Based on your own experiences or observations, list six concrete ideas that might help men and women communicate more effectively. For example:
   - If she asks, "Do you like this dress?" say...

   - If he says, "I'm going golfing and I'll clean the garage later," say...

   -

   -

   -

   -

"A Prairie Storm"

by Carolyn Arends

A young girl discovers that a simple prayer can have frightening consequences.

Page 56 in print book

1. At age four, Carolyn realized something was wrong, and tried to do something about it. What do you feel is the best way to include young children in what's happening without overly burdening them?

2. a) What is the first prayer you remember praying?

   b) Was your prayer answered?

   c) How can we teach children to pray so that it becomes natural to them?

3. Carolyn says there are "forces so ferocious in their power that—even if they bring you exactly what you need—they are likely to scare you silly" (page 59 in print book).

   a) Can you describe a time when you felt awe after a prayer was answered, perhaps in an unexpected way?

b) Can you think of an instance in which prayer (or the answer to it) changed *you*?

4. Perhaps you've had opportunities to pray with others in a group where prayers were answered.

   a) What do you remember as being the best thing about praying together?

   b) If you don't currently have the opportunity to pray with others, can you think of someone you could ask to pray with you? It could be in person, by phone or Skype, or even by email or text. You may need to get creative to find someone, but it's worth the effort.

5. 2 Chronicles 7:14 says, "If my people, who are called by my name, will humble themselves and pray and seek my face and turn from their wicked ways, then I will hear from heaven, and I will forgive their sin and will heal their land." What do you think might happen if we took these words seriously?

"The Neatness Wars"

by Eric E. Wright

The viewpoint of a husband who likes his things visible while his wife prefers everything neatly put away.

Page 61 in print book

1. In this story, the wife is organized in one way and the husband in another way. Have you ever shared a house, apartment, or dorm room with someone whose idea of organization was the opposite of yours? If so, how did you manage?

2. a) They say "opposites attract." What do you think?

   b) Can marriages or even business partnerships between polar opposites work?

   c) Can you think of some concrete ways in which two people can use their different perspectives to complement and help each other?

3. Neatness versus clutter is only one area of contention in a marriage.

   a) What other differences can create stress?

   b) Do you feel it's important to identify differences before you marry, or should you wait and deal with them as they come up?

4. Eric quotes from Colossians 3:13 (page 63 in print book). Is it possible to "bear with each other and forgive one another" without being seen as a wimp, becoming a doormat, or submerging your feelings until you explode?

5. What is the role of humour in relieving stress in relationships?

"What Your Sock Drawer Says About You"

by Sheila Wray Gregoire

Some thoughts on keeping priorities in mind and not becoming slaves to our possessions.

Page 64 in print book

1. Sheila talks about the time we spend looking after the "things" in our lives. Can you recall a time when it seemed that someone was judging you because of your appearance, possessions, decor, or tidiness?

    a) If so, describe what happened.

    b) How did that make you feel?

    c) How did you feel about the person doing the judging?

2. Can you think of a few times when you've caught yourself judging others for superficial reasons?

3. What are some ways we can counteract this tendency to judge others by appearances?

4. Do you think Christians can get too caught up in trying to show we have it all together?

5. What do you think God's priorities might be for your home?

"Faith, Hope, and Love: Give Them a Chance to Improve Your Health!"

by Denyse O'Leary

Why spirituality is good for your physical and mental health.

Page 66 in print book

1. Denyse says that volunteers who were taking placebos (fake medication) felt less pain than before, and people who had sham surgery actually got better (page 67 in print book). What was your reaction when you read this?

2. Perhaps you or someone you know recovered from an illness without the usual treatment.

   a) Can you remember what people said?

   b) To what did you attribute the recovery?

Discussion Guide for Hot Apple Cider

3. This article also discusses phobias and how they can be cured by Cognitive Behaviour Therapy. Denyse says "there is indeed such a thing as 'mind over matter.' And hope over fear" (page 73 in print book). Have you ever experienced something like this where you "retrained" your brain?

4. Denyse says that "Fifty years of medical research has established that people who follow a spiritual tradition usually have better mental and physical health" (page 74 in print book). How do you feel about this statement, and the other claims Denyse makes about Christianity in her article?

5. Have you seen evidence where God's love transcended illness or even death? Can you give an example?

"Nitroglycerin"

by Brian C. Austin

*A humorous look at the fact that many of us carry
vials of explosives around in our pockets.*

Page 75 in print book

1. Nitroglycerin is used medically to treat heart conditions such as angina and chronic heart failure. It's also used in gunpowder and dynamite.

   a) Did you know this when you read the poem?

   b) How would you interpret the poem?

2. There's an expression, "Laughter is the best medicine." When do you feel it's okay to laugh in the face of difficulties, and when does it show shallowness or lack of sensitivity?

3. We've all had a family member or friend who talks constantly about medical issues, sometimes repeating them detail by detail each time you meet, until you want to run and hide.

   a) In what ways does this encourage or discourage empathy?

   b) What are some ways you can share personal stories of adversity, especially stories you might be living in right now, without having people run for cover when they see you coming?

"Our Kids: Enemies, Allies, or What?"

by Ron Wyse

A *frustrated father struggles to understand his teenagers and himself.*

Page 76 in print book

1. What did you think of Ron's father's reaction when 17-year-old Charlie cut his hair after years of argument about its length?

2. Ron says, "I grew up with tension. Looking back, I can feel it rolled up tight in the pit of my stomach" (page 77 in print book).

    a) Can you relate to this feeling?

    b) What is frequently the cause of the tension?

3. Ron argues that parents and kids often don't realize the fight isn't against each other, but against spiritual forces (with kids and parents really on the same side).

    a) Do you agree or disagree with this concept?

b) How might this understanding affect the way we relate to other people in general?

4. Sometimes conflict is loud and angry and physical. Sometimes it's silent and remote and like a "cold war."

   a) What was your experience of conflict in your family?

   b) From your experience, can you think of a couple of practical ways to defuse conflict between two people?

5. Ron quotes several passages from the book of James. Two of them are:
   - "What causes fights and quarrels among you? Don't they come from your desires that battle within you?" (James 4:1 or page 80 in print book.)
   - "God opposes the proud but gives grace to the humble." (James 4:6 or page 82 in print book.)

   a) How does a parent model humility?

   b) What kind of an impact is made when a parent shows humility?

"Perspective"

by Mark Buchanan

A pastor ponders the difficulties we have in developing personal intimacy with imperfect people just like ourselves.

Page 86 in print book

1. Mark says, "I look back on all the 'best' friends I have had in my life, and most now are only a rubble of fading memories" (page 87 in print book).

   a) Can you relate to this, or have you found a way to retain your old friends even as you add new ones?

   b) Why do you think we lose touch, even with people who are important to us?

2. Mark urges us to "practise seeing others as new creations" (page 88 in print book). What are some practical steps we can take to do that:

   a) In our families?

   b) In our churches?

Discussion Guide for Hot Apple Cider

c) In our jobs?

3. Mark brings up the disagreement between Euodia and Syntyche from Philippians 4:2-3 (page 89 in print book).

   a) Can you think of a situation in your church or community where conflict between two individuals was handled well, and love was shown even in disagreement?

   b) While respecting other people's privacy, can you think of a situation where things weren't handled well?

   c) How might such a situation be handled differently in the future?

"What Was God Thinking?"

 ### by Brad Burke, MD

After losing his devout grandmother to breast cancer, a young doctor questions God's will.

Page 93 in print book

1. Brad is a doctor, so he knew better than most people what had happened with his grandmother. However, he still felt the timing of her death was unfair.

    a) Can you relate to his comment (page 95 in print book) that "suffering had moved from the theoretical to the touchable"?

    b) If you've experienced the loss of someone close to you, how did you deal with your emotions?

2. Many people blame God when bad things happen.

    a) Can you think of a difficult time in your life when you've asked, "God, what were you thinking?" or "God, did you forget about me?"

    b) If God responded to your question, what was His answer?

Discussion Guide for Hot Apple Cider

c) If God didn't respond, how did you react?

3. Brad says, "Some of my best patients were Christians, while some of my worst patients (and their families) who consumed my time—and my patience—were also Christians" (page 97 in print book).

   a) What kind of patient would your doctor say you are?

   b) How would you say your actions, when you are ill, reflect your beliefs about God?

4. Brad felt it was okay to be angry with God and to tell Him his frustrations. Do you feel the same way, or do you feel we shouldn't be angry with God?

5. Brad describes feeling a comforting hug from God (page 101 in print book). If you've ever felt something like that, how would you describe it?

"Hurtled into the Valley"

 *by Angelina Fast-Vlaar*

A recently remarried woman is told she has a malignant tumour.

Page 103 in print book

1. Angelina received a very tough diagnosis. How did she deal with it?

2. How did Angelina's belief in God soften the cancer diagnosis?

3. If you or a loved one received an unwanted diagnosis or experienced a serious disappointment:

   a) Did you feel hurtled into a valley?

   b) What helped you deal with the initial shock, and the subsequent results?

c) In what ways have you felt God's presence with you in the midst of difficult times?

d) How have others supported you or your loved one?

4. After reading this poem, what might you say to someone who has been diagnosed with cancer or some other serious disease?

"People Matter Most"

by Grace Fox

A reminder that people are far more important than possessions.

Page 105 in print book

1. What was your reaction to Grace's story about her mother-in-law's letting her son build a 16-foot sailboat in her living room?

2. Can you recall a time in your life when someone went to extraordinary lengths to show you that you mattered?

3. In past generations, families often kept an immaculate parlour which no one saw except certain guests.

   a) Have you ever visited a family whose house reminded you of a show home?

   b) How did you feel?

   c) What would you say is the middle ground between living in an expensive show home and living in a messy junkyard?

Discussion Guide for Hot Apple Cider

4. What are some other ways that we can teach our children that people are more important than money or possessions?

5. Can you think of a practical way we can show other people that they matter to us?

   a) A family member

   b) A neighbour

   c) An elderly person in a seniors' care facility

   d) A homeless person

6. Can you think of one way you could change your own home to make it more welcoming to others?

"Broken Bodies, Shattered Lives"

by Paul M. Beckingham

A missionary in Africa, dedicated to serving God, has a horrific car accident that leaves him brain-damaged.

Page 107 in print book

1. While most of us don't experience the kind of life-shattering accident that changed Paul's life, many people do have moments in their lives when they feel that God has abandoned them.

   a) Can you recall a time when you felt abandoned?

   b) Does that experience continue to affect your relationship with God, or has your relationship changed in some way?

   c) Describe an experience where you might have felt abandoned, but instead had no doubt that God was there with you.

2. Romans 5:3-6 says, "We also glory in our sufferings, because we know that suffering produces perseverance; perseverance, character; and character, hope. And hope does not put us to shame, because God's love has been poured out into our hearts through the Holy Spirit, who has been given to us. You see, at just the right time, when we were still powerless, Christ died for the ungodly."

   a) If you should encounter a situation where you feel powerless, do you think you could rejoice in it?

   b) How can reading about other people's trials help you trust God?

3. Paul offers seven ways we can learn fresh faith perspectives during loss or sudden change (pages 109 and 110 in print book).

   a) Which of these seven ways have worked for you?

   b) Can you think of additional ways?

"Be the CEO of Your Emotions"

 ## by Donna Carter

Tips for controlling our emotions instead of letting them control us.

Page 111 in print book

1. Donna says, "Our emotions are like warning lights on the dashboard of a car" (page 112 in print book). An intense emotion, that seems over-the-top for the triggering event, tells us that we need to deal with whatever underlying issue is causing the emotion.

   a) Can you think of a time when you or someone you know overreacted?

   b) What happened as a result of the overreaction?

2. Some negative emotions are anger, bitterness, depression, distrust, fear, frustration, grief, loneliness, and sadness.

   a) Which of these emotions are you most prone to feel without an obvious cause, or with only a slight one?

   b) What kinds of situations really push your buttons?

c) Can you detect a link between your strong emotional reactions and your past?

d) What can you do to reduce the intensity of your reaction when unsettling things happen?

3. Donna refers to King David's "unholy prayer" (Psalm 109 or page 118 in print book).

   a) What might lead you to talk to God the way David did?

   b) What happens if we tell God the truth about how we feel?

4. How would your life improve if you learned to manage your emotions better?

"Living Outside Our Comfort Zones"

by Eleanor Shepherd

After her son is paralyzed in a car accident, a mother realizes that a lifetime of adapting to change has prepared her for this moment.

Page 120 in print book

1. Eleanor says, "How I wished I could take my children and hold them close to me and keep them safe from all harm!" (page 120 in print book).

   a) If you could do this, who would you wish to protect?

   b) What are some coping strategies you've found that have helped you let go?

2. Eleanor's definition of comfort zones are "non-threatening environments, either places or situations, where we feel adequate and at ease psychologically and emotionally" (page 120 in print book).

   a) How would you describe a comfort zone?

   b) What is one comfort zone for you?

3. Eleanor's story recounts several incidents where she was confronted with significant challenges and felt pushed out of her comfort zone.

   a) Can you think of a few times when you were pushed out of your comfort zone?

   b) How did you feel at those times?

   c) In what ways did those occasions help you grow or fall back in your faith?

   d) What have you learned about yourself and/or God through these experiences?

4. When her husband became diabetic, Eleanor questioned God.

   a) Can you recall an occasion when you've questioned God?

   b) What was the response to your question?

"Dylan"

by Brian C. Austin

Reflections on the death of a newborn grandson.

Page 129 in print book

1. Brian writes from the perspective of a grandfather who believes that God is love, and that there is eternal life.

   a) How can you reconcile faith in a good God with the devastating loss of an innocent child?

   b) When a Christian experiences the raw agony of grief, should one's faith provide (or not provide) a cushion?

2. How much of someone else's grief do you think we can comprehend?

3. Romans 8:28 says, "And we know that in all things God works for the good of those who love him, who have been called according to his purpose." This verse is often quoted in the aftermath of tragedy.

   a) Do you think quoting a Bible verse such as this can be hurtful or helpful in the early days of grief?

Discussion Guide for Hot Apple Cider

b) When, or in what ways, might it be appropriate to share Bible promises that God will bring good out of their loss with people who are grieving?

c) In what other ways could you demonstrate the truth of God's promises?

4. The loss of an infant or a child feels wrong, unnatural. It tends to bring a very different grief from the loss of someone who has led a long, fulfilling life.

   a) If you've never experienced the loss of a child, how could you bridge the gap of understanding and empathy in order to relate to someone who has?

   b) What are some practical ways you could reach out to bring comfort to someone who has lost a child or had a miscarriage?

"How Big Is Your Umbrella?"

 *by Sheila Wray Gregoire*

After losing her newborn son, a young mother tries to understand God's role in her sorrow.

Page 131 in print book

1. In the midst of her second pregnancy, Sheila discovered that her baby had serious health issues. Twenty-nine days after his birth, he died.

    a) What does this comment of Sheila's mean? "I had never known what it was for a heart to truly break until that moment" (page 132 in print book).

    b) What did Sheila mean by the phrase "until that moment"?

    c) Can you relate to Sheila's brokenness, even in a small way?

2. Sheila mentions searching for "a reason for this storm" (page 132 in print book). She says that part of the problem in going through hard times is that we assume God must be trying to teach us something.

    a) When bad things happen in your life, do you believe God is trying to teach you something, or do you believe there could be something else going on?

b) Do you agree with Sheila that when bad things happen, it isn't always about us?

c) Can you share a time when God took an experience that was difficult for you and used it in an unexpected way?

3. Sometimes people try to bargain with God during difficult times.

   a) Can you recall a time you wanted to bargain with God?

   b) In contrast, describe an occasion when you've been able to trust God in the midst of a storm.

"Jesus' Disciple Wears a Stethoscope"

by W. Harold Fuller

A glimpse into the life of Dr. Aletta Bell, who moved to India in 1964 to help people, particularly Muslim women and children who weren't allowed to see a male doctor.

Page 136 in print book

1. "Unbelievable!" was the reaction of many readers after finishing this story. They hadn't realized that such conditions still existed in the latter part of the 20th century.

   a) Did anything here surprise you?

   b) If so, what in particular surprised you? For example: male attitudes? women's status? health conditions?

2. What were some of the effects of various non-Christian religions in this story?

3. Critics often say the gospel destroys other cultures.

   a) How would you describe the gospel?

Discussion Guide for Hot Apple Cider

b) In this true story, how did the gospel free the local culture from its own destructive tendencies?

c) Is there a way you might use the gospel more effectively in your culture?

4. Some people think missionaries focus only on winning converts while neglecting physical and emotional needs. In what ways did Dr. Bell disprove this stereotype?

5. Dr. Bell experienced the stress of frustration over unmet ambitions (pages 137 and 138 in print book).

   a) What personal spiritual experience brought peace to her?

   b) Can you relate to her frustration? If so, in what areas/ways have you found peace?

"Shards of Silence/ Seasons of Hope"

by M. D. Meyer

A delicate memoir documenting the healing of a woman who was sexually abused as a young child.

Page 147 in print book

1. The author shares her journey from childhood sexual abuse to healing. Were you surprised by the length and circuitousness of that journey? Why or why not?

2. When someone who should protect you hurts you instead, your ability to trust is damaged. How can family and friends help someone who has been abused learn to trust again?

3. Often a great deal of shame and unworthiness is associated with sexual abuse. But the shame is usually borne by the abused rather than the abuser!

    a) How can we reassure people who have been abused that we don't blame them for what happened?

    b) How can we build them up to know that they are worthy of love?

4. Multiple sources indicate that one out of every three or four girls—and one out of every five or six boys—will experience some form of sexual assault prior to age 18.

   a) Are you surprised by these numbers?

   b) What are the biggest needs of someone who has experienced abuse?

   c) How can communities or churches make it easier for people to share their experiences of abuse?

   d) What difference should it make if the abuser is a church or community leader?

   e) What can the church do to help an abuse victim understand that God is worthy of our trust?

Note: If there is an event in your past that you've kept hidden, please understand that sharing your story is the first step in the healing process. You might wish to talk about this experience with the group today. If not, commit to share it with a trusted friend or counsellor later.

Two places where you can find support:
Canadian Resource Centre for Victims of Crime. http://crcvc.ca/links
Rape, Abuse, and Incest National Network. http://www.rainn.org/get-help

"Crisis and Character"

by Paul M. Beckingham

The role suffering plays in molding our character.

Page 152 in print book

1. People often ask how anyone can believe in a loving God when there is so much pain and suffering in the world. The author of this article believes that God uses suffering to build character. Do you agree or disagree with him?

2. What do you think of his statement (page 152 in print book) "I need to see the preacher's scars"?

3. Paul quotes events from the life of the Apostle Paul, who suffered many things, but who wrote, "we also rejoice in our suffering..." (Romans 5:3 or page 153 in print book). Can you describe a time when you were able to rejoice in suffering?

4. After quoting Romans 5:3-5, the author of the story writes, "God gives us hope through suffering, renewing our sense of a future through crisis and pain" (page 153 in print book). How do you understand this?

5. The author quotes Rabbi Harold Kushner, who says that there are three sorts of people in the world (page 153 in print book):
   - "Those who dream boldly even as they realize that a lot of their dreams will not come true"
   - "Those who dream more modestly and fear that even their modest dreams will not be realized"
   - "Those who fear to dream at all, lest they be disappointed"

   a) Which type of person would you say you are?

   b) In what ways have you changed as you've grown older?

6. How has your character been molded through crises that you've faced?

Discussion Guide for Hot Apple Cider

"Searching For Something That Fits"

 *by Marcia Lee Laycock*

The folly of striving to find the perfect life.

Page 155 in print book

1. When you were young, where was your favourite hiding place?

2. If you've searched for the "perfect" thing to fill the void in your life the way Marcia searched for the perfect stone, share your experience.

3. Many people, not realizing that God already loves them exactly as they are, believe He won't love them until they somehow prove themselves worthy.

    a) Have you ever experienced a moment when you realized that God really does love you just as you are?

Discussion Guide for Hot Apple Cider

b) How did you feel?

c) What would you say to a friend who might not realize that God's love is unconditional?

4. Marcia says that God tells us to "remain" or "abide" in his love (page 156 in print book). In other words, there's nothing we can do to make Him love us any more than He already does.

   a) When are you most able to simply rest in God's love?

   b) Do you feel there are things you need to do, or change, so you're more worthy of His love?

5. How has God satisfied your longing to do something that makes a difference, or are you still seeking that?

"Friday, 8:50 a.m., April 7, AD 30"

by David Kitz

A retelling of the events surrounding the crucifixion of Christ, through the eyes of a Roman centurion.

Page 157 in print book

1. a) In this version of the story, how did the events come to life for you?

   b) Did you notice anything in particular that resonated with you or brought up questions?

2. The centurion Marcus is annoyed that the leaders—Pilate, Caiaphas, and Herod—could walk away, while he had to do the dirty work, whether he agreed with it or not. Does he have a point?

3. Along with the stained purple robe and the horizontal beam of the cross, Jesus carried "the weight of the world" (page 159 in print book).

   a) How do you understand this statement?

b) Do you think we bear personal responsibility for Christ's death, and if so, how?

4. Take a moment to reflect on how the author portrayed Barabbas in this biblical fiction (page 158 in print book). Then consider this statement at the top of page 162, "The response that a pardon can bring is well beyond understanding." What do you think this means?

5. The women who followed Jesus were present, but His disciples were absent from the procession that led to Golgotha. If this is true, what are the implications?

6. Marcus the centurion asked himself (page 157 in print book), "Justice? What justice was this?"

   a) Can you think of an instance where you witnessed someone being treated unjustly?

   b) What would God want us to do in such a situation?

"A Fertile Heart"

by Keturah Leonforde

A woman who is unable to have a baby reluctantly agrees to care for a newborn whose mother has been hospitalized.

Page 166 in print book

1. Keturah was willing to consult with others to find a solution which they could then implement; but she wasn't prepared to actively participate in the challenge of caring for the three-week-old baby.

   a) Can you relate to the way she felt?

   b) Do you understand how years of disappointment and bitterness can make someone appear to be cold and indifferent?

   c) What unanticipated blessings emerged as a result of this crisis?

2. Perhaps you have faced a crisis situation (your own or someone else's) where you had to step far out of your comfort zone.

   a) What role did your faith, or lack of faith, play in handling the situation?

b) Looking back, what qualities or resources did you discover, or tap into, to help you deal with the crisis?

c) Identify an important life lesson learned as a result of having gone through this crisis.

3. When you've had a need, who are some people who helped you even though it may not have been convenient or easy for them?

4. Many couples find themselves childless for one reason or another. How can friends and family be sensitive to their needs?

"The Joys and Surprises of Giving"

 *by Diane Roblin-Lee*

A woman reflects on times when she was blessed by giving away something she really wanted to keep.

Page 171 in print book

1. When so many people are in need, it can be difficult to decide what's appropriate and what's too much in terms of material wealth.

    a) What did you think of Diane's story of the fur coat?

    b) Is it wrong for people to want to look attractive?

2. Sometimes God asks us to do something for others in spite of the cost to us.

    a) Can you recall helping when it required a sacrifice on your part?

    b) If so, how did you feel afterwards?

3. Diane also had an amazing story about the house they bought.

   a) Can you think of a similar blessing you've received?

   b) When you are blessed, does the blessing belong to you alone? Why or why not?

   c) What is one way God has blessed you recently?

   d) How could sharing that blessing encourage someone else?

4. We often resist asking for help, yet others may not know of the need unless we tell them.

   a) How easy is it for you to share your needs with others?

   b) What is one need you currently have?

"Where Have All the Mothers Gone?"

 **by Thomas Froese and Jean Chamberlain Froese, MD**

An obstetrician strives to educate leaders in countries where women have a one-in-eight chance of dying in childbirth.

Page 181 in print book

1. Thom and Jean tell us that the equivalent of "three jumbo jets filled with pregnant women quietly crash to earth, every day—or 525,000 mothers every year" (page 187 in print book).

    a) How does reading these statistics make you feel?

    b) Why do you think there is so little media coverage of such a major story?

2. The issue isn't simply medical. It's actually cultural. What role does education play?

3. Can you think of other unfair situations women face simply because of their gender?

4. What are a few things even ordinary people could do to help make the world a safer place for women and children?

5. Thom and Jean had successful careers in Canada, but God placed the plight of these women on their hearts.

   a) Is there something you feel God has called you to do in order to make a difference?

   b) Have you been able to make progress in this area, or do you need help to carry out this vision?

   c) You may need a small support group to pray for you, help you plan, and hold you accountable. What are some steps you could take this week to share your vision with a few trusted friends?

"Mama Nellie"

by Paul M. Beckingham

Conversations between a missionary from Canada and his Kenyan housekeeper reveal amusing stereotypes.

Page 192 in print book

1. Paul's story about Mama Nellie reveals several cultural preconceptions. Can you describe a similar misunderstanding from your own experience?

2. Paul says, "A strange new angle of vision opened up for Mama Nellie" (page 194 in print book). Recall a time when you suddenly saw another person or group of people in a different light. How did you react?

3. A particular way of thinking may be just a misunderstanding, but it may also put others down or reveal racism.

   a) What are some types of jokes that really aren't funny?

   b) Is it ever okay to imitate someone with impaired speech or a disability?

   c) Do you have a standard you use to help you decide what is truly funny and what is destructive?

4. What message do churches or religious groups send if they promote such cultural misunderstandings?

5. What practical things could we do to counteract stereotyping or racism in our country, and help unite people?

"Will My Baby Die Without Me?"

 *by Grace Fox*

A missionary in a remote part of Asia gives birth to a child who needs complicated surgery.

Page 195 in print book

1. After Grace's baby was born with hydrocephalus, the newborn had to be flown to the United States for neurosurgery.

   a) How do you imagine Grace felt when she wasn't able to go with her daughter?

   b) What have you had to trust someone else with because you had no choice? How easy was it for you to rely on others?

2. Life is unpredictable. Recall a situation in your life where circumstances changed in a split second and you had to make a quick decision. How did you feel in that moment?

3. Where do you find personal strength when faced with difficult circumstances?

4. Grace mentions that God encouraged her through hymn lyrics she remembered (page 200 in print book). In what ways has God encouraged you in the past?

5. Grace had to trust the doctors and her husband to look after Stephanie, but ultimately she had to choose to trust God to look after all of them.

   a) How did trusting God change her perspective?

   b) If you have an issue you're struggling with, have you made a conscious decision to trust God with it?

"Jessie's Generation: Canada's Firebrands of Mercy and Justice"

by Jane Harris-Zsovan

The true story of Jessie Robinson, a well-to-do woman from Lethbridge, Alberta, who fought to help the poor and sick in the early 20th century.

Page 204 in print book

1. What did you think of Jessie's actions? How might they be different today?

2. Even though there are many poor people across North America, we aren't always aware of those close to home.

   a) Would you agree that those in our own country deserve our help first? Why or why not?

   b) If you think that people are poor because of circumstances beyond their control, or even bad decisions, how would you decide whether or not to help them?

Discussion Guide for Hot Apple Cider

3. Many of us feel bad when we hear about starvation and hopelessness in other countries. We may think we're powerless to do anything meaningful, but making an impact begins with one small step.

   a) Who do you know (usually a person of the same sex) who could benefit from some one-on-one time with you?

   b) Discuss ways to find a church, a local organization, or a global organization, such as World Vision, that needs volunteers in your area.

4. Jessie started out wanting to help one woman, and things grew from there.

   a) Do you know of other causes that started with just one small action?

   b) Can you think of one thing God has asked you to do, either in the past or recently, to help someone else?

5. How does Philippians 4:13, "I can do all things through Christ" (page 204 in print book), motivate us to move out of our comfort zones?

"How I Found Jesus in a Drug Dealer's Apartment"

by Deborah Gyapong

A young woman discovers God—the very God she had previously rejected—in a very unexpected place.

Page 210 in print book

1. We see from this story that God is faithful.

    a) What do you understand about God's love even for those who've turned their backs on Him?

    b) When have you felt God was reaching out to you?

2. Many people, including children, dabble in the occult without realizing what they're doing.

    a) Do you feel it's safe to do some things that have roots in occult practices, even if they seem benign?

    b) The author suggests doing this might open you to demonic oppression. What do you think?

3. The author says, "I wish I could say the rest of my life was perfect after my profound conversion" (page 215 in print book).

   a) How do you relate to this statement?

   b) Why do some Christians try to hide the fact that their lives aren't perfect?

4. The author says, "Despite a personal relationship with Jesus, I reserved the right to pick the parts of the Bible that 'spoke to me' and to ignore the rest" (page 215 in print book). Why does this habit of picking and choosing what to accept eventually create more problems?

5. The author mentions Neil Anderson's Steps to Freedom in Christ, a seven-step discipleship counselling process designed to help people resolve issues that are critical between themselves and God (page 218 in print book).

   a) In what ways would you agree or disagree that we're caught up in spiritual warfare between God and Satan?

   b) Where can we learn what it means to fight thoughts that don't come from God?

"Of Cobras, Culture and Change"

 by Don Ranney, MD
and Ray Wiseman

Two short stories based on the authors' real-life experiences as missionaries in India and South Africa.

Page 220 in print book

1. The missionaries in this story experience different forms of culture shock when they arrive in their new countries.

    a) Can you recall a time when you experienced culture shock of any kind? If so, how did you feel?

    b) How might churches and colleges prepare missionaries better for the cultural challenges they face?

    c) Read Acts 17:16-34, where Paul meets a cultural challenge. What can we learn from this?

2. These stories depict missionary work in the 1970s. How would you say the role of missionaries has changed since then?

3. The missionary appointees to both India and South Africa hint at possible tension between themselves and field leadership. (Note: This story is an excerpt from a book, *When Cobras Laugh*, that goes into more depth in this area.)

   a) Why are there interpersonal tensions within churches and other Christian organizations?

   b) In order to protect either the reputation of the Christian church generally, or the organization specifically, should internal problems be made public, or should they be kept quiet?

   c) Discuss the potential repercussions of deciding to remain quiet.

4. Have you experienced worship in a completely different cultural setting? If so, have your eyes been opened to new thoughts about worship?

"The Pink Blossom"

by Eric E. Wright

An elderly man wonders if he made a mistake in judgment years earlier.

Page 230 in print book

1. How do you interpret the end of this story?

2. Terrance and Susan made very different choices years ago.

   a) What fundamental difference distinguished the lives of Terrance and Susan?

   b) What results followed Terrance's choice?

   c) Susan's?

3. In what sense did Terrance have a "tarnished soul" (page 232 in print book)?

4. If you were Terrance, what would you do at the end of this story?

5. As you look at your own life, what choices have you made that reflect those of Terrance or Susan?

6. Does your current direction in life need redirection? If so, where could you begin?

"The Ventilation Grate"

 *by Brian C. Austin*

Memories rush back as a homeless person struggles through a cold night.

Page 233 in print book

1. The homeless exist in all societies, particularly in large cities. Society tends to see them as victims of unfortunate circumstances and bad luck, or as people lacking initiative. How accurate is this perception?

2. Homelessness often forces people to ask for money.

   a) Do you feel that giving money perpetuates the cycle of dependence, or is it needed aid?

   b) Proverbs 19:17 says, "Whoever is kind to the poor lends to the Lord." How do such verses apply in our day with government agencies and tax-supported relief programs?

c) In what ways does the potential for abuse (for example, money given for food but spent on alcohol) make it morally wrong to give money to people who may not use it wisely?

d) How can we give while minimizing the potential for abuse?

3. In Matthew 25:40, Jesus said, "Truly I tell you, whatever you did for one of the least of these brothers and sisters of mine, you did for me."

   a) How might we really be giving to Jesus by just stopping and talking to that person on the street?

   b) How is it possible to have a genuine friendship with a homeless person?

   c) What are some ways we can help someone in need live a fuller life?

Note: If you haven't read and discussed "One True Friend" (page 235 in print book), you may want to discuss it next.

Resources: There are excellent resources for understanding and helping homeless people at Street Level.

http://www.streetlevel.ca/resources/

"One True Friend"

by Donna Dawson

A teenage boy who's battling cancer and a homeless man help each other.

Page 235 in print book

1. Several readers have shared that they cried after reading this story. Why do you think people were moved?

2. Being a friend in need happens in different ways.

   a) Can you recall a time when you've interacted with someone living on the streets?

   b) What were your feelings before you approached (or were approached by) him or her?

   c) How did you feel after the exchange?

   d) Looking back, can you think of ways you could have helped that person?

3. Many practical ideas can help the plight of the homeless.

   a) What special needs do you see right in your own community?

   b) What online or local resources can you pass on? (For example, local shelters, foodbanks, clothing supplies, Alcoholics Anonymous, Narcotics Anonymous, medical support groups, bereavement groups, volunteer drivers, Meals on Wheels, home help.)

   Note: If you haven't already read and discussed "The Ventilation Grate" (page 233 in print book), you may want to discuss it next.

"Padre, Can I Have a Word?"

by Paul M. Beckingham

*A military chaplain challenges all of us
to really listen to other people's hurts and hearts.*

Page 245 in print book

1. Situations where someone refuses to listen to the concerns of people of lower rank or status can occur outside of the military. Recall a situation where a leader or group refused to listen to your input, even though your concerns were justified.

    a) How did you handle the rejection?

    b) In hindsight, do you wish you'd done anything differently?

2. It's easy to become angry with people like the foolish young captain in this story.

    a) What is the role of forgiveness in our day-to-day lives, whether from God, others, or ourselves?

b) Do you need to forgive someone, God, or even yourself, so that you can move on? What step can you take today?

3. In recent years, our society has become more and more aware of Post Traumatic Stress Disorder (PTSD) and its effects on individuals. In this story, Paul says that sometimes churches are places where people with battle scars seek healing.

   a) From your experience, would you say most churches are safe places for people to share hard things such as depression, anger, and suicidal thoughts?

   b) How could people in churches become more supportive concerning these issues?

   c) What other safe places could you recommend to someone in need?

"Shared Tears"

by Brian C. Austin

Words of advice for anyone wondering how to help a grieving friend.

Page 248 in print book

1. If you've read the poem "Dylan" (page 129 in print book), you know the author is offering advice based on personal experience. What was your impression of "Shared Tears"?

2. When someone we care about is grieving, most of us feel an almost desperate hunger to fix their hurt. Is it really more helpful to cry with them than to "offer wondrous words" (page 250 in print book), or is that a cop-out?

3. Can you recall a situation you've been in when "words of comfort" were just noise?

4. Most of us will agree that Scripture is truth. How can it ever be wrong to quote truth?

5. Shedding tears can bring intense embarrassment to many.

   a) What is an appropriate way to share the pain of someone else, and offer comfort, when the grieving party doesn't know how to let go and cry?

   b) If you're on the receiving end, how should you accept comfort from someone who can't or won't cry with you?

6. Our society tries to sanitize death (or "passing"), yet for many, the pain can be intense and raw.

   a) When we comfort another, how can we find a balance between offering reminders of the very real hope for eternity we find in Scripture, and acknowledging the almost bottomless hurt of grief in the present?

   b) Share some verses that have comforted you:
      - 2 Corinthians 1:3-4

      -

      -

      -

      -

"On Writing with Passion and Integrity"

by M. D. Meyer

*The author's reasons for writing—
or rather the impossibility of her not writing.*

Page 251 in print book

1. Although she herself isn't Aboriginal, the focus of much of M. D. Meyer's writing is on Aboriginal people who live in Canada's North. She says (page 252 in print book) that she "agonizes over the formidable task of telling their story... Do I dare speak for them?" And yet, she feels she must try.

    a) What are you passionate about?

    b) How does your passion motivate what you do each day?

    c) Could you be doing more?

2. Listening, without making assumptions, is a very difficult thing to do. It is perhaps made more difficult when wounded people find no one interested in what they have to say.

    a) How can we make ourselves available to people who are hurting?

b) How can we be more open to hearing uncomfortable stories?

3. "Integrity—being true to yourself and what you believe" (page 254 in print book). How accurate is this definition?

4. We've all been tempted to "throw in the towel" as the author did at one time. What are some concrete ways we could hold each other accountable so that we each follow our passions?

5. How did reading this piece open up new avenues of thought?

"My Letter to the Editor"

by N. J. Lindquist

A shy 12-year-old decides that God wants her to write a letter to the editor of her local newspaper telling people God loves them.

Page 256 in print book

1. What surprised you the most about this story:
   - That a 12-year-old would write something like this?
   - That N. J. found the clipping in her mother's purse?
   - That her mother never spoke about it to her?

2. Sometimes we go ahead and do something, simply because we feel we have to do it.

   a) When have you followed this urge?

   b) What was the result?

3. Sometimes we feel the need, but fail to follow through.

   a) Was there a time you really felt you should do something but you didn't do it?

b) Looking back, what might have been the result if you had done it?

c) Could you still do it now?

4. Many people who believe in God have difficulty sharing their faith with others.

   a) What are a few things that can keep you from sharing your faith?

   b) What would you say if you could share your faith in a natural, relaxed manner?

5. Think of something you feel you should do right now. If you are hesitating, what small steps could you take to begin to do it?

"The Child on the Tracks"

 *by Carmen Wittmeier*

The skepticism of her students leads a young college instructor to recall her experiences in a Romanian orphanage.

Page 260 in print book

1. Why might someone hesitate to participate in, or contribute to, humanitarian projects?

2. Discuss your reaction to Bob and his Bugatti.

    a) Is it fair to draw a parallel between Bob and the average North American?

    b) Would Bob's actions have been justified if he had parked 10 Bugattis on the track? What about 100?

    c) Would it make a difference if that child were his next-door neighbour instead of someone he didn't know?

d) Does Western culture place a higher value on a child in North America than a child in a developing country?

3. Carmen observes that rather than saving the child on the tracks (Gabriella), the child saved her.

   a) If you've helped a child through sponsorship or some other means, do you feel that getting involved has had a similar effect on you?

   b) If you can't relate to this story, has reading it created a desire for you to do something new?

"The Stuckville Café"

 *by Bonnie Grove*

A lonely waitress stuck in a small town wonders how God could possibly use her.

Page 266 in print book

1. Not by her own choice, Carol lives in a place she calls Stuckville. Her life seems to be a mess; yet other people are attracted to her. She says she wants to get a degree in psychology so she can help people (page 276 in print book). Carol says, "I pray for people. It's what I do" (page 273 in print book).

   a) Do you feel Carol needs/doesn't need a degree to help people?

   b) Have you ever known someone like Carol?

2. In the story, people seem to take extravagant liberties with each other's company. They stand close, ask personal questions, and keep coming back for more. Why are they able to do this and yet not offend or upset anyone else?

3. The story takes place entirely inside a small café. Other people come and go, but Carol always stays—she's always available.

   a) Do you feel you have a "Stuckville Café" in your life? If so, where is it and what happens there?

   b) If not, how could you either find a place where you might get help, or create a place where you might be a blessing to others?

4. Carol talks about "violent compassion" and "strange grace" (page 275 in print book). What do these two phrases mean to you?

5. Is there something you need to do before God can use you, or do you feel He's already using you in your current situation?

"The Clay and the Vine"

by Brian C. Austin

A reminder of the need to rely on God in everything.

Page 277 in print book

1. Surrender is implicit in the words of this brief poem. It's not a concept that fits well with independence and self-sufficiency. It doesn't sound nearly as strong and assertive as "commitment." What scripture supports surrender in a Christian's life?

2. The hero in a book or movie who takes a stand without backing down often stirs our admiration—but it may not be as easy to do in real life.

    a) Has there been an area in your life where you've taken a stand, but later fallen?

    b) If this has happened more than once, what does it teach you about yourself and about life?

c) What steps could you take to help you surrender in the future?

3. "Living the life He planned" (page 277 in print book) sounds like surrendering your identity and your will.

   a) If you've experienced times of surrender to God, in what way were you less yourself?

   b) Was there something in the surrendering that you wish you could preserve—or wish you could forget?

4. As you come to the end of this book, do you feel your heart has been stirred to rely more on the God who made you who you are, or your soul warmed by the realization that the God who created the world loves you?

Acknowledgements

Thanks to the contributors to *Hot Apple Cider* for sending initial question suggestions for their stories.

Thanks to Marguerite Cummings for editing the questions in this book with me, for assistance with the front and back pages, for creating the "Reader's Guide for Hot Apple Cider," and for never getting tired of proofreading.

Thanks to Wendy Elaine Nelles, co-editor of *Hot Apple Cider*, who contributed to the front and back pages and our style guide.

Thanks to A.A. A. Adourian and Claire Alexander for help with copyediting and proofreading.

N. J. Lindquist

A Second Cup of Hot Apple Cider

If you enjoyed *Hot Apple Cider*, you'll want to read the second book in this series, which has 51 stories of hope and encouragement.

Trade paperback and digital books

- Bestseller—this uplifting inspirational anthology has more than 45,000 print copies in circulation
- 2013 Book of the Year Award from The Book Club Network, Inc.
- Winner of the 2012 Christian Small Publishers Gift Book Award
- Winner—13 awards (6 first-place awards and 7 awards of merit) in the 2012 The Word Awards

"Sometimes all you need is a reminder that there is something good in the world."

—*Midwest Book Review*

"Some books surprise you with their ability to take your breath away.... Be sure to buy more than one, for you will probably have the urge to share this gem of a collection with others."
—*Faith Today*

There is also a ***Discussion Guide for A Second Cup of Hot Apple Cider*** which offers helpful resources for readers, book clubs, small groups, or speakers.

Trade paperback and digital books

Available from most bookstores and online

http://hotappleciderbooks.com

Hot Apple Cider with Cinnamon

67 stories of finding unexpected love by 61 writers

Trade paperback and digital

"In these pages you will find tales of love—love for a parent, for a friend, for a stranger—that span Canadian hockey rinks and African villages and Philippine homes. You will find people choosing hope in the midst of a panicky Alberta hospital room, choosing God in the midst of Alzheimer's, choosing peace in the midst of losing a child.... The stories in this book will help you choose love. Every time."

—from the foreword by author Sheila Wray Gregoire

Winner, four The Word Awards

Available from most bookstores and online

http://hotappleciderbooks.com

A Taste of Hot Apple Cider

16 heart-warming stories and poems from 15 writers

Trade paperback and digital

"Through poems, fiction, and nonfiction alike, [the writers] remind readers that the struggles we face are common to everyone. Their honest descriptions of wrestling with cancer, caring for and losing aging parents, dealing with a spouse's dementia, moving beyond one's fear to tell neighbours about Jesus, and more, show us that hope is very much alive."

—from the foreword by author Grace Fox

Discussion Questions Included!

Available from most bookstores and online

http://hotappleciderbooks.com

Index of Authors and Discussion Pages

Carolyn **Arends**	A Prairie Storm (p.22)
Brian C. **Austin**	Nitroglycerin (p.30) Dylan (p.48) The Ventilation Grate (p.80) Shared Tears (p.86) The Clay and the Vine (p.96)
Paul M. **Beckingham**	Broken Bodies, Shattered Lives (p.42) Crisis and Character (p.56) Mama Nellie (p.68) Padre, Can I Have a Word? (p.84)
Paul H. **Boge**	Blind Date (p.18)
Mark Buchanan	Perspective (p.34)
Brad **Burke**, MD	What Was God Thinking? (p.36)
Donna **Carter**	Be the CEO of Your Emotions (p.44)
Keith **Clemons**	Faith of Our Mothers—Holy Faith (p.12)
Donna **Dawson** (Fawcett)	One True Friend (p.82)
Angelina **Fast-Vlaar**	It Was Then That I Carried You (p.10) Hurtled into the Valley (p.38)
Grace **Fox**	People Matter Most (p.40) Will My Baby Die Without Me? (p.70)
Jean Chamberlain **Froese**, MD	Where Have All the Mothers Gone? (p.66)
Thomas **Froese**	Where Have All the Mothers Gone? (p.66)
W. Harold **Fuller**	Jesus' Disciple Wears a Stethoscope (p.52)
Sheila Wray **Gregoire**	Romance Amid Reality (p.20) What Your Sock Drawer Says About You (p.26) How Big Is Your Umbrella? (p.50)

Bonnie **Grove**	The Stuckville Café (p.94)
Deborah **Gyapong**	How I Found Jesus in a Drug Dealer's Apartment (p.74)
Jane **Harris-Zsovan**	Jessie's Generation: Canada's Firebrands of Mercy and Justice (p.72)
David **Kitz**	Friday, 8:50 a.m., April 7, AD 30 (p.60)
Marcia Lee **Laycock**	An Almost Silent Friendship (p.16) Searching for Something That Fits (p.58)
Keturah **Leonforde**	A Fertile Heart (p.62)
N. J. **Lindquist**	The Diamond Ring (p.14) My Letter to the Editor (p.90)
M. D. **Meyer**	Shards of Silence/Seasons of Hope (p.54) On Writing with Passion and Integrity (p.88)
Denyse **O'Leary**	Faith, Hope and Love: Give Them a Chance to Improve Your Health! (p.28)
Don **Ranney**, MD	Of Cobras, Culture and Change (p.76)
Diane **Roblin-Lee**	The Joys and Surprises of Giving (p.64)
Eleanor **Shepherd**	Living Outside Our Comfort Zones (p.46)
Ray **Wiseman**	Of Cobras, Culture and Change (p.76)
Carmen **Wittmeier**	The Child on the Tracks (p.92)
Eric E. **Wright**	The Neatness Wars (p.24) The Pink Blossom (p.78)
Ron **Wyse**	Our Kids: Enemies, Allies, or What? (p.32)

Keep in Touch

If you want to know about new books, where and when our writers are speaking or signing, special offers, webinars, and more, please connect with us!

Like us on Facebook

@hotappleciderbooks

Follow us on Twitter

@thatslifecomm

Visit our website

http://thatslifecommunications.com

or http://hotappleciderbooks.com

Publisher

That's Life! Communications

Books that integrate real faith with real life

That's Life! Communications is a niche publisher committed to finding innovative ways to produce quality books written by Canadians with a Christian faith perspective.

> http://thatslifecommunications.com

We'd love to hear your comments about this book or any of our other books. Please post a comment on our website or write to us at:

> comments@thatslifecommunications.com

www.ingramcontent.com/pod-product-compliance
Lightning Source LLC
Chambersburg PA
CBHW050506120526
44588CB00044B/1623